Locomotion Papers

THE

DARTFORD LOOP

LINE

R. W. Kidner

THE OAKWOOD PRESS

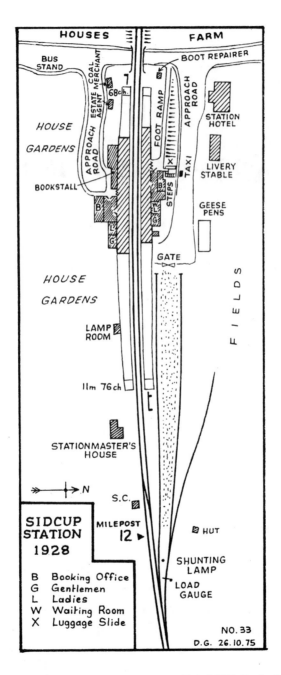

SIDCUP
STATION
1928

B   Booking Office
G   Gentlemen
L   Ladies
W   Waiting Room
X   Luggage Slide

NO. 33
D.G. 26.10.75

ISBN 085361 090 8   *First Published 1966. Revised 1982.*

Railway travellers in general seldom question the mysteries of the railway way of life, and probably few users of the "Loop Line" have paused to wonder why their line bears this title, when it appears on the map as only one of three equally-important lines joining London and Dartford. The answer is that when planned, it was in truth a loop line, leaving the South Eastern Railway's long-established North Kent line near New Cross and proceeding by a southerly route, avoiding the built-up riverside area, to join the same line just west of Dartford. The completion of the New Main Line through Orpington in 1868 (opened as far as Chislehurst in 1865) and the much later opening of the third route to Dartford via Bexleyheath (and still later the Lewisham loops), somewhat obscured the original character of the Dartford Loop.

Why was the Loop Line built? There were a number of reasons; it offered a slightly more convenient route to Gravesend and beyond; as Greenwich and Charlton were not yet joined, the Dartford trains had to use the more circuitous route via Blackheath. It is also probable that the South Eastern directors, already conscious of the growing threat from the London Chatham and Dover Railway, saw in the new line a way of filling a void which the "Chatham" might at any moment decide to fill themselves.

The South Eastern already had complete possession of the riverside area of North Kent (it was not until 1886 that the "Chatham" managed to reach it at Gravesend), and the nominally-independent Mid-Kent Railway, under S.E.R. auspices, with its recently-opened extension to Addiscombe Road, gave them the Surrey border country. In the very large square of territory bounded on the north by the North Kent, the south by the South Eastern Old Main Line, on the west by the Mid-Kent and on the east by the South Eastern's line from Paddock Wood through Maidstone to Strood, the L.C. & D.R. Main Line was the only occupant.

And so, forestalling any expansionist ideas in the other camp, the S.E.R. promoted in 1862 its Bill (25-6Vic.Cap.96) dealing with "Tunbridge and Dartford Lines". The Act was relatively uncomplicated. It stated that "Railway No. 1" (the New Main Line) should commence at or near the junction between the North Kent and the Greenwich; that "Railway No. 2" (the Dartford Loop, though not so named in the Act) should commence at a point on the line of No. 1 in the parish of Lewisham; and the existing line between the junction of the Greenwich and the North

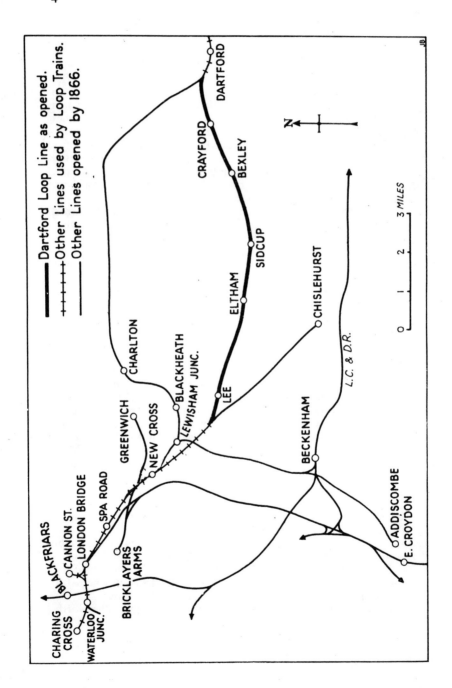

Dartford Loop Line as opened.
++++ Other Lines used by Loop Trains.
Other Lines opened by 1866.

CHARING CROSS
BLACKFRIARS
CANNON ST.
WATERLOO JUNC.
LONDON BRIDGE
SPA ROAD
BRICKLAYERS ARMS
GREENWICH
CHARLTON
NEW CROSS
BLACKHEATH
LEWISHAM JUNC.
LEE
ELTHAM
SIDCUP
BEXLEY
CRAYFORD
DARTFORD
CHISLEHURST
BECKENHAM
ADDISCOMBE
E. CROYDON
L.C. & D.R.

N

0   1   2   3 MILES

Kent and the crossing of George Street Deptford, could be widened on the north side. Whoever drafted the Act had also worked in powers to acquire extra land at Bricklayers Arms, Maidstone, and North Camp (Aldershot) stations, without attempting to show any relevance with the main purpose. The Act further stated that the new railway No. 2 should be regarded as part of the North Kent Railway and could automatically charge tolls as if it were part of that railway originally. It seems that construction must have begun at Dartford Junction, because the 6″ O.S. map for 1865 shows only a portion of about 1 mile extending west from that point. However, apart from a deep cutting between Bexley and Sidcup, there were no engineering difficulties, and the line duly opened on 1st September, 1866.

After leaving the newly-built Chislehurst line at a lonely junction, now Hither Green station, the first station was Lee (subtitled "for Burnt Ash" in deference to a then important village). The double-line spur to the west of the station, leading into Hither Green marshalling yard, was added on 30th April, 1905 (not used for passengers). The line now continued through rolling fields to a point some way south of the important village of Eltham, where a station of that name was set up, although it lay in fact within the confines of Mottingham. At what was later New Eltham (opened 1878 as Pope Street, renamed New Eltham and Pope Street 1886, and New Eltham 1927) it passed under the Sidcup Road, and again took to the country to pass nearly a mile north of Sidcup, the station of that name being in the parish of Lamorbey. The necessity for the line to descend to sea level before reaching Dartford forced some fairly heavy cutting between Sidcup and the next station, Bexley, where the siting was close to the village. At Crayford the line reached the Thames Marshes, passing under the Rochester Road and joining the North Kent line to run into Dartford station, precariously perched on its brick viaduct which has since frustrated a much-needed expansion of this station.

Even at the opening of the line, Dartford was very much built up and the planner obviously had difficulty siting the station between the town and the marshes. The site chosen, bounded on the north by the Phoenix Paper Mills pond, on the west by a road, and on the east by the River Darent, has allowed only limited extension beyond the meagre requirements sufficient when it was simply an intermediate station on the North Kent line. By moving the embankment closer to the mill-pond at some time after 1866, a Down relief line and a third platform face were obtained. By removing the locomotive turntable at the Down

A *

DARTFORD

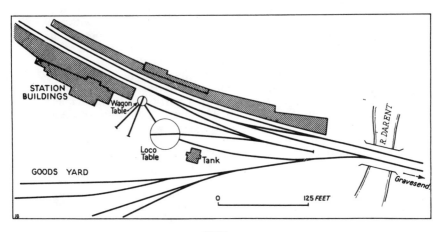

1866

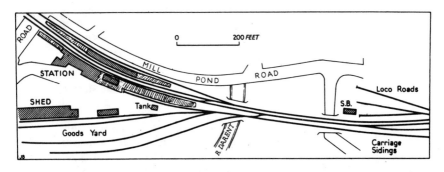

1910

end (Up side), probably when the locomotive sheds were opened at nearby Slade Green, the Up platform was considerably lengthened. In addition, a third line was laid from Dartford Junction into the station. Judging from signals in old photographs it seems that all platforms at Dartford were always signalled to start trains in the Up direction, but between the crossovers and Dartford Junction, the southernmost line was, as it now is, only Up, and the other two only Down.

The timetable with which the line opened gave eleven stopping trains per day, and one fast, in each direction. As evidence that the Loop Line was seen as an escape route byepassing the North Kent line, five of these were Maidstone trains and four were for Strood. After the line was opened, most of the North Kent line trains terminated at Dartford. But obviously there was some reaction from North Kent line travellers, for a few years later many of the through trains were back on the North Kent table, and most Loop Line trains were terminating at Dartford.

Q class

There are no precise records of the types of locomotives and rolling-stock used in the early years, but they were probably a fairly mixed bag. Although J. A. Cudworth has been in charge of South Eastern locomotive matters for twenty-one years, he had only recently brought out his standard E class 2–4–0 and I class 0–6–0, and a secondary line like the Dartford Loop would have had to manage with rebuilt relics of Benjamin Cubitt's régime (even some of the earliest Forrester and Sharp engines were still around).

Internal squabbles on the S.E.R. Board, resulting in unsuccessful classes being produced by R. C. Mansell and even by the General Manager's nephew, A. A. Watkin, kept the railway short of adequate locomotives until the early eighties, when James Stirling began to bring out in large numbers his Q class 0–4–4T, O class 0–6–0 and F class 4–4–0, all of which were standard motive power on the Loop Line until electrification, along with the later Wainwright D and E class 4–4–0, C class 0–6–0 and H class 0–4–4T.

The carriages used until the turn of the century were short four-wheelers, some with framing outside the body and some with matchboard sides. They were mainly made up into "sets" with short buffers except at the ends of the "set". The prevalence of these coaches, tiny by comparison with some of the Northern lines, was due to the fact that many North Kent trains worked through the Metropolitan Railway tunnels to stations on other railways north of London, and owing to the steep grades between Borough Market Junction and Farringdon and particularly when passing under Holborn , locomotives could not haul coaches of heavier weight.

1870 SER 3rd class carriage

For the next few years it seems that north-west Kent remained relatively unpopulated, for the widely-separated stations of New Cross, Lee and Chislehurst were considered sufficient to cater for the traffic offering. On 1st November, 1871, however, a station was opened at Grove Park, a mile south of the junction between the Loop Line and the New Main Line, and on 1st June, 1873, St. John's station was opened, at the point where the Main and Loop Line diverged from the North Kent. Nevertheless it was not until 1st June, 1895, that Hither Green was opened, at the divergence of the Loop from the Main Line. The layout on the Loop side of the station embodied a middle up through line with no platform; there seems little point in this unless the Up platform was to be used as a lay-by for a "branch" train, but it does not appear that Hither Green was ever used as a terminus or that fast trains ever overhauled slow ones. This through road was used for non-stopping Up trains, however, until abolished in the thirties.

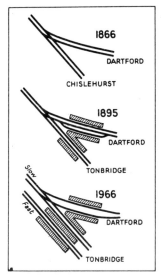

Hither Green

During the next thirty years, as the social status of places like New Cross and Camberwell declined, professional people working in London tended to move farther out, and big comfortable villas were built at places offering a good train service to London. At Sidcup, the area immediately south of the station, Station Road, Longlands Road, and Hatherley Crescent, became built up, bringing new season ticket traffic to the line, most of it second class rather than third. Somewhat cheaper houses were built at Lee and New Eltham. Eltham station, however, attracted little building until much later. With the increasing population, good coal-order businesses were built up around the goods yards, and although the opening of the electric tramway to London from Eltham may have taken some passengers (a 2d. fare to London was some attraction), the Loop Line maintained quite satisfactory traffic. The other tramways in the district, the Bexley Council Tramways and Dartford Light Railways, which operated jointly after a fire destroyed all the Dartford rolling stock, had little effect, as the line ran through Bexleyheath rather than Bexley, and only touched the Loop at Crayford station.

The South Eastern Railway in this period had seen much change. In 1898 the ruinous competition with the L.C. & D. came to an end when a Joint Committee was formed to operate both lines, under the title of S.E. & L. & C.D.R., later simplified the "South Eastern and Chatham Railway". The Joint Committee was faced with a rapid growth in its coastal traffic, both the Boat Train side and to the holiday resorts, and in 1903–4 doubled its main line down as far as Orpington. This made Hither Green a six-platform station, the new lines lying to the south of the former ones. Also, on 1st May, 1895, a new line, known as the Bexleyheath line, had been opened from Blackheath to just west of Dartford Junction. This had little effect on the Loop Line, except that a new station called Well Hall was opened in Eltham, making the title of the Loop Line station even more of a mis-nomer. (It was altered to Mottingham on 1st October, 1927.) On 1st October, 1902, an additional station on the way into London was added, Southwark Park, between New Cross and Spa Road: this was closed on 15th March, 1915, though the platforms remained for another twenty years.

l class

The coming of the 1914–18 War changed things, of course. The attractive locomotive livery of the S.E. & C.R., green with red and yellow lining, was replaced by a drab grey, with enormous white number on tender or tank. Also munition factories were set up around Crayford and Dartford. The Vickers-Maxim works just east of Crayford had rail access, and a private branch nearly a mile long was built from the main factory to two large workshops on the marshy ground between Crayford and the viaduct carrying the Bexleyheath line. This branch was worked by Vickers' own engines.* There also ran on it a curious vehicle made from the underframe of an ex-LSWR carriage with a petrol engine mounted at one end: a kind of rail lorry which apparently did not have much success. This remained derelict on a spur until the last War. This branch is now removed, but the girder bridge that carried it over the river is still there.

*A 0–6–0ST Hunslet 1882 reb. 1918 (3661) withdrawn 1930.
 B 0–4–0ST Walker Bros. reb. 1919 (3345) sold 1941.
    0–4–0ST Peckett (1758) 1929 (from Erith Works 1932).

It should be mentioned here that other sidings were established at Crayford, though precise dates cannot be assigned. They were:

(a) Crayford Brick Siding, a quarter of a mile west of the station, protected by a signal box of the standard S.E.R. pattern (not a ground frame). A trailing connection from the up line led through a cross-over layout to a long siding and a locomotive shed for one engine, and by another reverse a line led up a steep gradient and across a three-arch brick viaduct, to some sandpits to the south of the railway. The locomotive (Hunslet 0–4–0ST) propelled one or two wagons up to the end of the siding, where they were filled by means of tip wagons on Decauville track leading on to a staging, and were drawn down again some days later, for attention by the Loop Line pick-up goods working. The whole siding was laid in second-hand S.E. and L.C. & D. chaired track. It was pulled up in 1931.

(b) Crayford Waterworks (south side) siding. The pumping station to the north-east of the station had no siding, but that to the south-west had a short spur leading through an iron gate

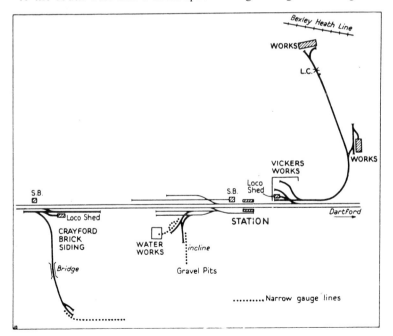

to a point where a narrow-gauge line ran alongside, for transferring the coal or coke to the boiler-house. This siding was worked by S.E. & C.R. engines propelling in.

(c) Dartford Heath gravel pits. A line ran round a steep curve just west of the station to a loading-ramp, from which a rope-worked incline carrying a narrow-gauge railway ran up to a large gravel pit on the edge of Dartford Heath. This siding was also worked by S.E. & C.R. locomotives propelling in, with much squealing of tortured tyres: it has now been lifted and largely obscured by spoil.

The War also brought much ambulance train traffic, for a large military hospital was set up north of Sidcup village, fed from Sidcup Station. The casualties came in grey-painted converted S.E. & C. and L. & S.W. stock with large red crosses on the sides, and were met at the station by Crossley and Ford ambulance cars. A bizarre note was struck by the fact that the Ford driver had no nose: this was before the days of plastic surgery.

After the war, the standard of punctuality on the Loop, along with other S.E. & C. lines, was very poor. Many of the trains were hauled by F or B class engines, which with their seven-foot driving wheels were not very suitable for stopping train work. The Loop Line is not really heavily graded, but the pull up from Bexley was tiring for a heavy train (1/100 from Bexley to Albany Park, then 1/165); even the 7.59 a.m. fast from Sidcup, always on Fi working, would pass through both New Eltham and Eltham at barely more than a walking pace. The morning and evening business trains were getting rapidly heavier, and were now often hauled by a C or a O class 0–6–0, which were certainly not capable of high speeds, but were better at getting away from a stop.

In 1923 the ramshackle empire of the Joint Committee was merged with the L. & S.W.R. and the L.B. & S.C.R. to form the Southern Railway. Talk of electrification in the London area, which had been heard before, but led to nothing in view of financial problems, now became more definite. The Southern plan was a far-reaching one, envisaging within a few years the electrification of all lines within fifteen miles of London. There were already electric services on the A.C. overhead system on a small part of the L.B. & S.C.R. and on the D.C. third-rail system on a small part of the L. & S.W.R. The experts decided on extending the latter system; the Eastern Section (as the former Joint Committee's lines became) was to be converted first as regards the line from Victoria to Orpington (converted 12th July,

An Up train at Sidcup about 1903; the engine is a Watkin 2-4-0 as rebuilt by Stirling (Dewey, Sidcup).

Bexley station with an Up train entering hauled by F class 4-4-0 No. 24.

New Eltham station about 1914.

Special strawberry train in Bexley sidings about 1908; Q1 class 0-4-4T No. 134.
(Collection D. Hood)

An interesting day in Sidcup siding, 23 April 1930; visiting steam crane 80S lifts a long length of steel trunking off a bolster wagon; below, the load leaving the yard behind a Sentinel steam-lorry.

C class No. A693 passing a Dartford-Gravesend local train laying by in Crayford sidings with R class 0-4-4T No. A671, 30 April 1930.

An evening fruit train passing a Down electric train just east of Sidcup on 24 July 1931; E class 4-4-0 No. A36.

Port Victoria excursion near Sidcup on 9 June 1930; F1 4-4-0 No. A206 with mixed 6-wheeled and bogie stock.

01 class 0-6-0 No. A 384 removing a wagon from the waterworks siding at Crayford on 1 Sept. 1930.

The Crayford Brickworks engine outside its shed on 10 April 1929.

Electric train made from SECR steam stock passing the new overbridge under construction for the Westhorne Avenue extension near Mottingham in January 1935.

Albany Park station under construction in May 1935.

The disused 'rail-lorry' outside the Vickers Great War annexe at Crayford, 30th April 1930.

Coal empties from Northfleet passing Sidcup in December 1972; class 47 leading a class 45 (T. Burnham).

New platforms 1 and 2 at Dartford; 16.17 Loop Line to Charing Cross (left), 16.12 North Kent to Cannon Street (right); 20 Oct. 1975 (D. Gould).

A 10-EPB train leaving the reversing siding at Sidcup for the 17.14 fast to Charing Cross, 26 Sept. 1975 (D. Gould).

1925); the turn of the Dartford lines came a year later, being advertised to start on 12th July, 1926, although due to the Coal Strike a restricted service of electric trains was operated for a short while from 6th June. Test trains had in fact run daily since the early spring.

Between Lee and Mottingham an extra earth-return rail was laid between the running rails, but the rest of the branch had only the normal third (positive) rail.

The "new" electric trains were masterly examples of the art of conversion: they were in fact old steam stock on new frames. The first trains comprised four coaches with the two end ones motored, but one of the trailer coaches was cut out at an early stage to improve performance. However, at peak hours two extra trailer coaches were formed between two three-coach sets, thus giving eight coaches. Although in 1926 some entirely new metal-panelled stock was built, on the same lines, the conversion of steam stock remained the policy for suburban sets, the rebuilders taking in turn steam stock from all three former Companies (and at a later stage some former elevated-electric stock). All types of train ran at times on the Loop (except for some two-coach trains designed for the South London Line); the main difference was that stock made out of S.E. & C.R. steam stock had seven "firsts" in the centre coach, whereas that made from L.B. & S.C. and L. & S.W. steam stock had the "firsts" divided between the trailer and one motor car.

From 1929, all trains carried square boards on the side of each motor coach detailing main stopping points; these were kept in racks on the platforms at termini and changed as required by porters; the practice ceased some six years later.

Converting the trains themselves was, however, not enough. The signalling system was still antedeluvian. In rush-hour conditions often near to chaos the trains groped their way from one manually-operated box to another: New Cross A and B, North Kent East, Southwark Park, Spa Road, London Bridge A and B, Borough Market, Metropolitan Junction, Union Street, Waterloo A and B, Belvedere, and finally into Charing Cross. Electric colour-light signalling must be the answer, and this was begun, between Charing Cross and Borough Market, on 27th June, 1926, being complete to Hither Green by 30th June, 1929, (but not to Sidcup until 4th February, 1962).

The effect of the new signalling was to speed up the service generally, allowing more trains to run, and the service on the Loop Line was increased in rush hours, although the half-hourly service sufficed in the middle of the day. These midday trains were three-car only, and the other five coaches were left in the platforms at Charing Cross or Cannon Street all day. Some steam trains continued to run; although Cannon Street locomotive shed was closed, there was very little diminution in the number of steam engines to be seen in London, and indeed the three western-most platforms at Charing Cross were not at that time electrified. Gradually, however, a time-table emerged whereby the only steam trains down the Loop were fast from London Bridge to Dartford. In view of this, an extra panel was put into the train-indicators at London Bridge, lettered "Via Gravesend", and referring to any train by way of any of the three lines to Dartford, which was not stopping. Before this innovation, an arrow would appear against the Dartford Loop panel even for a train not stopping at any Loop Line station.

By 1930, the introduction on the Main Line of the Li class 4-4-0, and on the former L.C. & D. Main Line of the King Arthur and Lord Nelson 4-6-0 classes, had released many of the D and E class 4-4-0s, and these began to operate on fast Loop Line trains. The more powerful Di and Ei rebuilt classes never came on the Loop, except for a short period when on some foggy days (then more common than now) a morning corridor train from Ramsgate would be diverted through the Loop stopping at Sidcup only, and this was hauled by one of the rebuilds, also including in its formation the Pullman Car Cosmo Bonsor, then running in dark red livery.

Six-wheeled coaches disappeared after electrification (except for Excursions), and steam stock comprised either standard SE & C R 'sets' with characteristic raised guards look-outs at each end, or old LSWR and LBSC bogie vehicles, with a liberal mixing-in of six-wheeled vans.

A recurring problem which affected the Loop trains was the tendency to flooding in the tunnels between St. Johns and New Cross. A heavy Spring thundershower could bring the water over the running rails, and though this was no problem in steam days, it was serious when the line was electrified. On at least one occasion (in 1928) the section was switched out and rush-hour trains were propelled through the floods by C class goods engines brought up from Bricklayers' Arms. After 1930 improvements in drainage of the trackbed were made to overcome the trouble.

At this time the Loop Line stations still had a very rural appearance. From Crayford station the view of open fields to Bexley was only marred by the recently-opened Dartford bye-pass bridge; from Bexley the attractive view across the marshes to the Cray was unspoilt (and is even today!), although from 1926 the electrical sub-station immediately east of the cutting stands out like a sore thumb (there was another sub-station at Eltham). At Sidcup, Up trains could be seen approaching across a vista of fields, and a hundred yards beyond the station open country began again, for Longlands Road was only built up on its south side. Eltham and Lee were also still on the outskirts of development, and at Hither Green the locomotive depot was not yet built, the land on the Up side being an enormous rubbish-dump, only just recovered from a decade of mysterious smoking, probably caused by spontaneous combustion of rubbish, but alleged by some to be the result of a Zeppelin bomb. A network of uneven sidings for stabling ballast vehicles covered this open ground, and here could be seen the orange-painted coaching antiquities in which ballast crews were carried: four-wheelers dating back in some cases to the sixties.

Sidcup station may be taken as typical of the former South Eastern Railway's provision for passengers. There was a booking office both sides, and no footbridge or tunnel (the present footbridge was added only recently). Anyone who wished to change platforms must go down the approach into Station Road, under the bridge and up the other side. On the Down side the platform was above road level, and a wooden slide was provided, down which baggage slid to the waiting "Outside Porter", who would deliver trunks to your home on his handcart for a few pence. At the foot of the ramp on the Up side waited the East Surrey Traction Company bus: until 1926 a dark blue Daimler, but later a red AEC K-type, since the Company had been absorbed into the "General" network. The solid-tyred wheels were always well "chocked" to prevent the bus from running down the hill, and when it started it had to be "swung", a feat which usually drew a few onlookers. Occasionally the crew would gingerly squeeze the bus under the low railway bridge and retire for a long turn-round in the Station Hotel.* Incidentally, the Sidcup down distant signal was a particularly hard "pull", being sited 1,378 yards from the box.

A feature of the sidings on the Loop was they had no head-shunt, and the engine shunted actually on the running line, presumably no problem when there was only one train per hour. Recently, with the much increased service, a long head-shunt* has been constructed at Sidcup.

The journey to London was then rather more colourful. In the middle of the day, or a Saturday evening, one would pass the L.M.S. and L.N.E.R. goods trains on their way to Hither Green via Metropolitan Junction and London Bridge (a service diverted when the Lewisham Loops were opened) as well as Great Eastern trains coming up from the East London Line. Beyond North Kent East Junction there were the empty coast trains shuttling back and forth from Rotherhithe Road to Charing Cross and Cannon Street, with their train engine at the rear and one or two H class tanks leading. And there was always a chance to see a grand old "Gladstone" 0–4–2 on the turntable outside the Brighton side at London Bridge. There were many more "specials" of various sorts: Race Specials for Folkestone or Tattenham Corner, Hoppers' Specials crammed with vociferous East-enders, Territorials Specials, sometimes with gun-limbers on match-trucks at the rear.

There was plenty of variety too on the Loop itself. Not only were there seven classes of locomotive in regular use (Bi, E, D, Fi, 4–4–0, Oi and C 0–6–0 and H 0–4–4T), but there were also special workings. During the Kentish soft fruit season there was a daily Up fruit train, composed of every kind of van the traffic department could lay its hands on, including G.W., L.M.S. and L.N.E.

The Station Hotel, Sidcup, was demolished in 1975. The head shunt at Sidcup was taken over for the new reversing loop.

stock, and sometimes the odd S. & D.J.R. van in blue livery.
On Sunday there were weekly steam excursion trains to the Kent
Coast, usually comprising sets of fourteen six-wheelers of S.E. or
L.C. & D. origin, which stopped at all stations. For a brief period
in the early thirties some of these started from the long-disused
Bricklayers Arms terminus.

After 1930, the character of the Loop Line changed rapidly.
Building was going on apace, particularly to the south of New
Eltham and between Sidcup and Bexley. Overcrowding increased
to the point where something radical must be done, and since
the barrier to a more frequent service was the heavy occupation
of the lines from St. Johns to London, it was an obvious answer
to use the newly-opened Lewisham Loop and put in a service to
Holborn Viaduct, over a line which had no passenger traffic from
Lewisham to Nunhead, and comparatively little from Nunhead
to Cambria Junction (Loughborough).

The former L.C. & D. branch to Greenwich Park, which
crossed the Loop Line trains' route at St. Johns, had been
derelict since 1st January, 1917; by building a north loop from
the Main Line to the Mid-Kent (the south loop had been opened
a year after the Dartford Loop), and another from Lewisham
Junction to the disused branch, it had been possible from 7th
July, 1929, to run goods trains from Hither Green via Lewisham
to Nunhead on the former L.C. & D. line. On 16th July, 1933
electric trains began to run over the first-mentioned loop to
Lewisham and on to St. Johns, and on 30th September the same
year a service began over the second loop, thus providing an
extra peak-hour service from the Loop Line via Lewisham,
Nunhead and Cambria curve to St. Pauls and Holborn Viaduct.
These trains, which carried as a headcode U in place of the usual
L, stopped only at Nunhead (sometimes) and Peckham Rye after
leaving the Loop but nevertheless took some nine minutes
longer to reach Holborn Viaduct than the normal trains did to
reach Cannon Street. Possibly for this reason, they were poorly
patronised, and loading was only 2 or 3 persons per compartment.
Some terminated at St. Pauls' (renamed Blackfriars in 1937).

From 7th July, 1935, a fresh load of commuters to swell the
traffic came from the new station of Albany Park* between Sidcup
and Bexley. This served a large housing estate then being built
on what had been ploughed fields: one of the first examples of an
entirely new suburb as against extensions of old suburbs.

New electric train stock continued to come into service,
but whereas the trains for the out-of-town services, such as

* Albany Park: This station was shown on a London Transport map of
  1934 as "Claremont Park" (the name of another nearby housing estate
  of the 'thirties).

18

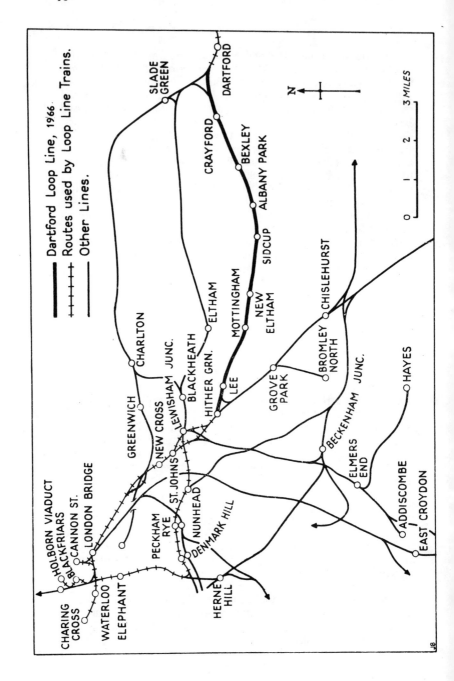

Dartford Loop Line, 1966.
Routes used by Loop Line Trains.
Other Lines.

N

3 MILES
0   1   2

SLADE GREEN
DARTFORD
CRAYFORD
BEXLEY
ALBANY PARK
SIDCUP
NEW ELTHAM
MOTTINGHAM
ELTHAM
LEE
HITHER GRN.
BLACKHEATH
CHARLTON
GREENWICH
LEWISHAM JUNC.
NEW CROSS
ST. JOHNS
GROVE PARK
CHISLEHURST
BROMLEY NORTH
BECKENHAM JUNC.
ELMERS END
HAYES
ADDISCOMBE
EAST CROYDON
HOLBORN VIADUCT
BLACKFRIARS
CANNON ST.
LONDON BRIDGE
CHARING CROSS
WATERLOO
ELEPHANT
PECKHAM RYE
NUNHEAD
DENMARK HILL
HERNE HILL

Brighton and Portsmouth, were entirely new, the stock for the Eastern Section continued to be built up from former steam stock. From 6th July, 1930, electrification had been extended from Dartford to Gravesend, and some Loop trains went through to Gravesend.

The last electrification project to be completed before the war—to be the last for another twenty years in fact—covered the various routes to Chatham and Maidstone. From 2nd July, 1939, therefore, electric trains for Maidstone West and Gillingham began to use the three lines between London and Dartford. The majority used the North Kent, but some did use the Loop, and for the first time semi-corridor electric stock appeared on this line, and steam services practically ceased.

The outbreak of war in September 1939 brought a heavy cut in services initially, but after a period of confusion, running settled down on a scale somewhat below the pre-war level, interfered with occasionally by enemy action at the London end. The Blackfriars and Holborn service was withdrawn (restored on 12th August 1946) First-class was abolished within the London Transport area on 7th October, 1941.

When the full force of A.R.P. came to bear upon the railway, conditions of travel became somewhat wearisome. In the early days, all trains had to stop during an alert; lighting was reduced and drawing of blinds at night enforced. The plastic sheets pasted over windows to prevent them splintering, with a small diamond shaped hole in the centre, made quick identification of stations (now without name-boards) difficult for a weary worker just awoken from a doze. However, there were plenty of bomb-stories for passengers to swap, even though the more dramatic events always seemed to be on some other line. After the short sharp era of the daylight raids came the long years of the night raids, and finally the deadlier appearances of the flying bombs, one of which caught the line near Southwark Park, blowing out of the three northernmost running lines. One piece of damage which had a long-term effect was the destruction of Blackfriars signal box; when in March 1946 a Question was asked in the House of Parliament about the restitution of the Loop Line services to Holborn, the answer was that this could not be done until the difficulties caused by the loss of this box were overcome.

A curve completing the triangle at the junction of the Loop and the North Kent west of Dartford was opened on 11th October, 1942. This is not a true chord, but runs parallel to the Loop before joining it, to allow a long train to fit in section between the two signal boxes, Crayford Spur A and B. Although some development work on new rolling stock was being carried out, only ten new sets for the whole suburban service were introduced between 1939 and 1946. It is not surprising therfore that by the end of the war, when the line came to restore full service there was a shortage of serviceable stock. Cannibalisation began to take place, and various coaches were inserted in the three-car sets to strengthen them to four coaches. No regard was taken of origin or roof-height, and some sets included coaches of L. & S.W., S.E.C. and L.B.S.C. origin, giving a very untidy appearance. The very oldest L. & S.W. sets, dating back thirty years, had had their coach-lengths increased before the war, and were converted to four-car sets during the war. Some of these were now being broken up, and their unusual trailer coaches with former first-class saloon, now demoted to second, could be found on a few Loop Line trains. Since the seats were disposed around the four sides of the saloon, one had the opportunity of travelling sideways, which at any rate made a change. Some new all-welded metal trailers were also coming out and being mixed into the sets: nevertheless there were still many three-car motored sets as well as two-car trailer sets on the go, and a peak hour train might at any time comprise six, seven or eight cars; with no advance information, crowds at London Bridge had to do some scuttling when a "sixer" appeared.

In the hard winters of 1940, 1944 and 1946 there was much trouble with icing and snow. There was no de-icing trains running at this time. Frozen points meant that stock was unavailable in the mornings, and coated conductor rails caused trains to stall. One day in January 1947 Loop passengers waiting at London Bridge were astonished to see several electric trains coming in from East Kent with steam pilot engines still attached. When snow was falling, the real trouble started late in the evening, when the short trains came on. The snow would pack under the collector shoes, reducing speeds to a jerky 10 m.p.h. (and this accompanied by blinding flashes which lit up the North Kent sky); in such conditions if a short train had to pass a point where there was a long gap in the conductor rail, it might well stall for lack of momentum. On some days eight-coach trains were kept running even off-peak, for with four collector-shoes, stalling was unlikely, though the pyrotechnics were in no way diminished.

Soon some entirely new six-a-side four-coach sets began to appear. The first sets had rounded ends, but in 1946 the now-familiar square roof-end became standard. Although in the first few sets all coaches were compartment type with some wide compartments for "firsts", later ones had at least two coaches of the open variety, losing twenty seats per coach, but giving more mobility and better standing. A pair of double-decker trains (strictly $1\frac{1}{2}$ decks) came out in 1948; this idea to cope with the rapidly increasing crush failed because the top deck could not be cleared quickly enough at stations. The legs of people in the top deck compartments were fitted in between the heads of the people below, and access was by a short stairway in the centre of one of the downstairs seats. With a full complement of twenty including standing in the lower compartment, and eleven sitting above, the exchange of passengers at London Bridge took well over the twenty seconds allowed. These sets only worked briefly on the Loop, before going on to the Bexleyheath for regular working. They were not followed up: the decision was taken to opt for ten-car trains of traditional stock instead, and orders for platform lengthening and two-car motored sets were put in hand. All platforms were lengthened by 1955.

In 1949 an attempt was made to clear up the appearance of the old suburban sets by marshalling coaches of the same origin together (e.g. all four coaches ex-L. & S.W. or all ex-L.B.S.C.). Gradually these wooden coaches with their letter head-codes began to disappear; the ex-S.E. & C.R. stock, still with S.E.R. monogram on the luggage-rack brackets, soon became a rarity, the coach interiors (though not the frames) having put in some sixty years of service. The ex-L. & S.W. sets and the 1926 steel-panelled stock lasted some years longer.

In 1948 the Express Dairy installed a compressor plant on the Down side at Mottingham, served by rail-born milk tank wagons.

In 1957 work began away down in the heart of Kent on electrifying the remaining steam services (diesel locomotives were still rare visitors) and by 9th October, 1961, all lines still open were electric, except the Tonbridge–Hastings and Ashford–Hastings, which were diesel. With the closure of the time-honoured steam locomotive depots at Tonbridge, Gillingham and elsewhere, the chance of ever seeing a steam engine on the Loop dropped to nil. Under the policy of concentrating freight movements the sidings at Bexley and New Eltham were removed: those on the Up side at Lee went when the platforms were lengthened.

The Loop Line settled down to a future of increasing overcrowding alleviated by the few possible steps that could be taken to increase frequency: few because with only four lines into Cannon Street and two through Borough Market to Charing

Cross, serving six heavy commuter routes, nothing but a programme of major engineering at the London end (and indeed at Dartford) could substantially allow more trains to be run.

As part of its job of carrying the Loop Line's commuting thousands, the Southern has always paid great attention to playing about with the timetable. Some branches have a virtually uniform table, but never the Loop. In the late twenties, each new issue of the local tables, then issued free by Smiths the printers in Sidcup High Street, had the impact of high drama, as various trains were added, accelerated or decelerated. Since then the service has become more stable, but complexity still exists. In the 1962 tables, for example, there were over a dozen different workings:

Head Code	Train originating at	Calling at
42/43	Gillingham	All stations
40/41	Dartford	All except Hither Green, St. Johns, New Cross
40/41	Dartford	,, ,, St. Johns
42/43	Gillingham	,, ,, Hither Green, St. Johns, New Cross
46/47	Crayford	,, ,, St. Johns
44/45	Gravesend	,, ,, Albany Park, Hither Green, St. Johns
46/47	Crayford	,, ,, St. Johns and New Cross
42/43	Gillingham	Only at Albany Park, Sidcup, Bexley
46/47	Bexley	,, ., Sidcup, Lee, Hither Green
50/51	Dartford	All stations via Lewisham
54/55	Gravesend	,, ,, ,, ,,
		(Some terminating at Cannon Street and others at Charing Cross.)
58	Dartford	All stations except Nunhead and Denmark Hill to Holborn Viaduct
58	Dartford	All stations except Nunhead and Denmark Hill to Blackfriars
58	Crayford	All stations except Nunhead and Denmark Hill to Holborn Viaduct
58	Dartford	All stations except Albany Park, Mottingham, Nunhead and Denmark Hill to Blackfriars

Headcodes: even numbers to Charing Cross, odd to Cannon St. Not used above: 52/53 Gillingham via Lewisham; 56/57 Sidcup or Crayford via Lewisham.

Prior to 1917, the SE & CR used an elaborate system of headcodes, devised in SER days, making use of six different headboards placed in a variety of positions on three lamp irons on the buffer beam and one at the chimney. The Loop headcode was a square board with white background and horizontal black strip, placed at the chimney. After 1917 only white discs and a disc with a black cross were used, and in the SR days two extra lamp irons were fixed at each side of the smokebox, giving six positions and enabling only white discs to be used. At night, in SECR days, white and green lamps were used in various combinations.

Additional Notes to Reprint

Since this book was first published in 1966, some progress has been made in adapting the line for increased traffic. In 1967, £50,000 was allotted for the building of a new siding at Sidcup, allowing trains to reverse there more easily, being an electrified loop on the Down side, Down end. On 1st November, 1970, a new power signalbox was opened at Dartford, replacing all boxes on the four routes to London. Dartford station was rebuilt 1972-73 to replace the Up platform and station building by an island platform. The present arrangement thus consists of two island platforms connected to a new (rather temporary looking) booking office by a covered footbridge. Although improving train working (especially with the increased freight traffic), it is doubtful if the new station is much better for the passenger.

On the rolling stock side, the original S.R. 4-SUB sets were phased out from early 1954, and the normal train comprised two 4-EPB sets and a 2-EPB set, while through trains beyond Gravesend were formed of 2-HAP or 4-CEP corridor sets; 4-VEP units began to arrive in March 1975. The experimental PEP train of 10 coaches worked over the Loop from 20th August, 1973, to 7th September, 1973; the smoothness of riding was appreciated by the passengers, but not the paucity of seats.

Freight traffic: Although no trains now stop, this is undoubtedly much heavier than ever before. Traffic includes: Block oil tank trains, to/from Hoo Junction, for grain refinery; block gypsum trains, Mountfield Sidings (British Gypsum)—Northfleet APCM sidings; block coal trains, Welbeck Colliery (for example)—Northfleet APCM. These last usually comprise 43 45-ton (loaded) hopper wagons, and are double-headed by Midland Region locos, either 2 class 47's or a class 47 and a class 45. All other freight trains worked by class 33 or class 73 (electro-diesel) locos.

General freight includes reinforcing rods from and scrap to Sheerness Steel, Queenborough, individual cement wagons, ballast trains to/from Hoo Junction.

Track: Much of the track has been relaid with continuous welded rail and concrete sleepers in recent years.

A number of road over-rail bridges have been rebuilt in recent years. These include bridges at Mottingham (Court Road), New Eltham (Avery Hill Road), Albany Park (Bexley Lane) and Crayford (London Road).

Dartford resignalling: The number of existing signal boxes replaced is variously stated. Those eliminated on the Loop were Mottingham, Sidcup, Bexley, Crayford, Crayford Spur B and Dartford Junction. One effect of the resignalling has been the installation of Solari indicators on the Up platforms of Loop Line stations, showing destinations of first and second trains.

Crayford station was rebuilt using a CLASP system prefabricated booking office probably around 1967.

Hither Green partially modernised in March 1972.

1957 Frequency Conversion Scheme: In connection with the conversion of the power supply to 50 cycles/sec., new rectifier sub-stations were built at Hither Green, New Eltham, Albany Park and Dartford Junction. The two latter used the old buildings. The sub-station at Mottingham was demolished.

Collision at Bexley: On 12th November, 1970, the 21.03 Charing Cross-Dartford was standing in Bexley station when it was run into in the rear by a freight train. No one was injured; the freight train driver jumped clear just before impact. The Inspecting Officer, Lt.-Col. Townsend-Rose, attributed the accident to the freight train driver's failure to control his train properly on the falling gradient from Sidcup.

Ten car scheme: 10 car trains were introduced on the following Loop Line services from 13th June, 1955:

Dartford-Charing Cross: 7.09, 7.25, 7.48, 8.42.
Charing Cross-Dartford: 16.23, 17.52, 18.16

Ten car trains were introduced on the remaining rush hour Charing Cross services and on Cannon Street trains from 4th March, 1957. When the line was resignalled for the 10 car scheme, the Walker one-wire block telegraph was replaced with BR standard 3-position interlocking block. Other routes to Dartford had Sykes block.

Dartford No. 1 box was abolished in 1954 and the work was described in the *Railway Gazette* for 25th June of that year. This included transferring its work to No. 2 box, with power operation of points and signals on the London side of the station, track circuiting of all roads from Littlebrook to Dartford Junction, installation of new BR block at Dartford and Dartford Junction and the complete relocking of the lever frames. New Eltham signal box was replaced by an electrically released (from Sidcup) ground frame for the Up siding.

Dieselisation: During the early 1960's the Loop Line pick-up goods was worked by a 350 h.p. 0-6-0 diesel shunter from Hither Green, one of the 1949 Ashford-built batch, 15211-15236. For a couple of years before the goods yard was closed, a class 33 Bo-Bo diesel electric was used.

Sidcup reversing siding: Trains were reversed at Sidcup before this was installed. A footbridge was built (enabling the Down side booking office to be closed), an Up starter (semaphore) was provided on the Down platform, and a trailing crossover laid in on the Up side of the station. In addition to reversing trains, the loop is sometimes used to allow one passenger train to overtake another (to restore the correct sequence) and, occasionally, for a passenger train to overtake a freight.

Other sidings: The six sidings at Mottingham have been reduced to one, which is normally clipped out of use and is used only in emergencies. The siding at Crayford is still regularly used to store empty block cement trains. A ground frame is provided at Crayford.

Freight traffic continued at a significant level although a decline in cement production at Northfleet resulted in shorter coal trains (often hauled by single Class 56 locomotives from 1979) and the run-down of the BP Grain oil refinery oil traffic. However, continental train ferry wagons appeared more frequently. Track magnets were installed for the BR standard automatic warning system (aws).

A derailment on the Up side of Mottingham on 11 October 1977 caused considerable disruption to traffic. A wagon of a Northfleet coal train became derailed and struck a Northfleet-Dunstable cement train. The two Class 33 locomotives and several bogie cement wagons of the Dunstable train fell down the embankment, resulting in considerable damage to back gardens.

From 1st June 1981 off-peak passenger services were cut to half-hourly after about 19.30 on Mondays to Fridays and all day on Saturdays as an economy measure and Albany Park station was closed on Saturday evenings.

(Above notes supplied by Mr. T. G. Burnham)

Mr. Richard Davey, who was working at the locomotive depot at Slades Green in SE & CR days, has sent some interesting notes. There was an early train from Dartford at 3.45 a.m. *via* the Loop Line, which terminated at St. Johns. This is believed to have been a connection with the 4.20 a.m. Plumstead to London train. The stock was worked empty from St. Johns to Rotherhithe Road, and the crew picked up a fresh train to work 6.15 ex-New Cross *via* the Bexleyheath line. On this early train, he and his fireman, Harry Eves, usually on Q class No. 95, often encountered thick fog, which necessitated keeping the firehole door shut to make it possible to pick up the signal lights. "The engine had to be thumped nearly all the way to Lee".